Practical
Karate

Defense Against
Armed Assailants

Practical
Karate 4

Defense Against Armed Assailants

M. Nakayama
Donn F. Draeger

Tuttle Publishing
Boston • Rutland, Vermont • Tokyo

Library of Congress Catalog Card Number: 98-87646
ISBN 0-8048-0484-2

DISTRIBUTED BY

NORTH AMERICA
Tuttle Publishing
RR 1 Box 231-5
North Clarendon, VT 05759
Tel: (802) 773-8930
Tel: (800) 526-2778

SOUTHEAST ASIA
Berkeley Books Pte. Ltd.
5 Little Road #08-01
Singapore 536983
Tel: (65) 280-3320
Fax: (65) 280-6290

JAPAN
Tuttle Shokai Ltd.
1-21-13, Seki
Tama-ku, Kawasaki-shi
Kanagawa-ken 214, Japan
Tel: (044) 833-0225
Fax: (044) 822-0413

First edition
07 06 05 04 03 02 01   00 99 98   10 9 8 7 6 5 4 3 2 1

Printed in Singapore

TABLE OF CONTENTS

AUTHORS' FOREWORD

THERE is perhaps no greater disservice to man than the creation of false confidence in his ability to defend himself. Whether this false confidence is manifested in his nation's armed might, or his own personal ability, the result is the same, though of different proportions, when tested—*disaster!*

The current *karate* boom in the U.S.A. has instilled in many would-be experts a serious, false sense of security. This is the natural outgrowth of a human psychological weakness. Everyone wishes to be physically fit and able to defend himself and his loved ones from danger and quickly turns to any sure-fire guarantee of such abilities.

Unscrupulous and unqualified self-appointed *karate* "experts" daily exploit this human weakness and prey on an innocent, unsuspecting public. This grossly perpetrated fraud is based on the quick learning of ancient mysterious Oriental combative forms such as *karate,* and almost always makes its appeal colorful through the use of adjectives such as "super," "destructive," "terror tactics," and guarantees you mastery of an art that will make you "fear no man." All such get-skillful-quickly schemes should be carefully investigated before taking them seriously, for true *karate* involves constant dedication to training and is never a short-course method. Choose your instructor carefully.

On the other hand, authentic teachers of *karate* do exist in the U.S.A., and their teachings have full merit. These teachings are deeply rooted in traditional, classical *karate* and require a liberal application of patience and regular training to develop expert *karate* skill. There are various schools that stem from historic Oriental antiquity, all of which

7

are legitimate and have both merits and shortcomings. The choice of which school to follow can be decided upon only by the interested party.

The average person is confined to a daily life that requires of him a heavy investment in time and energy in order to earn a living. Leisure time is generally at a minimum and it is spent at less enervating pursuits than classical *karate* practice, a demanding and rigorous "pastime." But the need for a practical system of self-defense designed for the average person is more evident than ever before. Police files give mute testimony to the increasing number of robberies, assaults, and other vicious crimes.

In self-defense situations involving armed assailants, either single or multiple, each situation is extremely dangerous and more complex than any type of unarmed attack. Accordingly, *karate* techniques must be learned thoroughly and executed as automatic responses to any series of happenings, if serious injury is to be avoided.

Like its predecessors, Books One, Two, and Three, this book is a categorized collection of self-defense situations and recommended *karate* responses. It is written for every male person and brings to him a chance to improve his personal self-defense abilities without engaging in the severe discipline and dedication to daily training required by classical *karate*. It is not an exhaustive survey of *karate* methods, but it contains methods that give direct consideration to easy learning for the average person. All methods described in this book are workable *karate* self-defense responses based on meeting single and multiple armed assailants. The responses are simplified, direct methods of self-defense. Because of their complexity and the inherent dangers connected thereto, razor and gun defenses have not been included in this volume. If you have already studied and practiced the necessary *karate* fundamentals found in Book One of this series, the situations in this volume will be easy to learn. Otherwise, after reading about the situations and responses herein you may find it necessary to turn to Book One, the fundamentals book, and find the necessary movements and practice exercises that are required to make these responses work effectively.

The reader is reminded that even complete mastery of what is outlined in this text *will not* give the possessor of that mastery invincibility in personal encounters. However, it will certainly better prepare him for common eventualities likely to be encountered in situations requiring the defense of his life or that of others. He is further reminded that mere reading and one or two rehearsals of each response in this book will not produce effectiveness.

The authors are indebted to the Japan Karate Association for the use of their facilities and hereby acknowledge with pleasure the assistance of those members and officials who have made this book possible. Additional thanks are due to Kazuo Obata, whose excellent photographic skills have contributed greatly towards the easy readability of this book; to Barclay Henderson, William A. Fuller, C. Nicol, and George Hoff, students of combative arts, whose posing for the "assailants" parts of this text has been invaluable.

Tokyo, Japan

M. NAKAYAMA

DONN F. DRAEGER

PREFACE

KARATE is a martial art developed by people who were prohibited the use of weapons, thus making it a *defensive* art. When one is attacked, the empty hands (which the word *karate* implies) are quite sufficient to defend oneself if one is highly skilled in the art. However, to become highly skilled takes exacting discipline, both mental and physical. The main purpose of this series of six books is to avoid the advanced techniques of *karate* which require many years of study and instead to describe simplified *karate* technique as easy-to-learn responses to typical self-defense situations.

Karate is highly esteemed as a sport, self-defense, and as a physical attribute for athletics in general. It is becoming increasingly popular in schools, offices, factories, law enforcement agencies and the armed services, varying in degree as required by the respective wants and needs.

In response to the many requests for treatment of *karate* purely as a defensive system, it is hoped that the information contained in this series of six books will be more than sufficient to meet these requests. In conclusion, if readers of this series of books will fully understand the principles and ideals of *karate*, taking care to use its techniques with discretion, they will reflect great credit to this magnificent art.

Zentaro Kosaka

ZENTARO KOSAKA
Former Foreign Minister
of Japan
Director, Japan Karate Association

11

THE FIRST and most complete and authoritative text on *karate* in the English language, titled *Karate: The Art of "Empty Hand" Fighting*, by Hidetaka Nishiyama and Richard C. Brown, instructor and member of the Japan Karate Association respectively, made its appearance in 1960. It presents *karate* in its three main aspects—a healthful physical art, an exciting sport, and an effective form of self-defense. As such, it is considered the standard textbook of the Japan Karate Association and adequately serves both as a reference and instructional manual for novice and expert alike.

Many students of *karate* find the study of classical *karate* somewhat impractical in modern Western society, chiefly because time limitations prohibit sufficient practice. These students generally desire to limit their interpretations of *karate* to self-defense aspects. With this sole training objective in mind, a series of six books is being prepared which describes in simplified form the necessary *karate* movements for personal defense that can be learned by anybody of average physical abilities.

The authors, Mr. Nakayama, Chief Instructor of the Japan Karate Association and Donn F. Draeger, a well-known instructor of combative arts, bring a balanced, practical, and functional approach to *karate*, based on the needs of Western society. As a specialized series of *karate* texts, these are authentic books giving full and minute explanations of the practical art of self-defense. All movements are performed in normal daily dress and bring the performer closer to reality.

Today, *karate* is attracting the attention of the whole world and is being popularized at an amazing rate. I sincerely hope that this series of books will be widely read as a useful reference for the lovers of *karate* all over the world. It is further hoped that the techniques shown in this series of books need never be used by any reader, but should an emergency arise making their use unavoidable, discretion in application should be the keynote.

MASATOMO TAKAGI
Standing Director and
Head of the General Affairs
Department of the Japan
Karate Association

12

Practical
Karate

*Defense Against
Armed Assailants*

ESSENTIAL POINTS

1. Never underestimate your assailant. Always assume he is dangerous.

2. Stepping, weight shifting, and body turning are the keys to avoiding an assailant's attack and bringing him into position for your counterattack.

3. Turn your body as a unit, not in isolated parts, for maximum effect.

4. If the ground is rough, bumpy, or slick, you may be unable to maneuver as you would like. Simple weight shifting and twisting of your hips may be all that is possible. Don't get too fancy in your footwork.

5. Your body can only act efficiently in *karate* techniques if you make it a stable foundation, working from braced feet and a balanced position as you deliver your blow.

6. Coordinate your blocking or striking action to the assailant's target area with your stepping, weight shifting, and body turning for maximum effect.

7. Do not oppose superior power with power, but seek to harmonize it with your body action and direct it to your advantage.

8. Seek to deliver your striking actions to the assailant's anatomical weak points (vital points) rather than to hard, resistant areas.

9. After delivering the striking action to your assailant's target area, you must never loose sight of him and you should be constantly alert for a continuation of his attack.

10. Use discretion in dealing out punishment to any assailant. Fit the degree of punishment to the situation.

Chapter One
CLUB AND STICK ATTACKS

ASSAILANTS armed with clubs or sticks often attack with single- or double-handed grippings, making use of overhead, backhand, diagonal, or haymaker strokes as well as jabbing, poking, or blocking tactics. These methods in combination can be used with extreme effectiveness against an untrained person. Occasionally, assailants working in pairs or small groups will use the weapon-holding assailant to distract the intended victim while one or more of the others of the group effect a sneak attack. This situation is often reversed, that is, the unarmed assailants will distract while the armed ones sneak attack.

Being attacked by an assailant using a club or stick or an object used similarly, requires a proper response by you if you wish to avoid serious injury or even death. The situations are extremely complex and dangerous and may allow you no mistakes.

The person expertly trained in *karate* techniques is able to meet such situations with confidence, *but not without difficulty*. Keeping that in mind, you as an average citizen must develop appropriate responses as shown in this chapter. They have been prepared for your capabilities and to cover the minumum necessary principles to effectively meet common eventualities connected with armed single and multiple assailants.

All responses described in this chapter must be practiced with partners. Begin slowly, so that you have complete knowledge of what you are trying to do. Gradually speed up the attack situations and your responses in meeting them. Seek to build an automatic response by frequent daily practices several times a week.

Practice in normal daily garb and do not limit yourself to smooth, flat surfaces such as a gym floor. Try to practice on grass, gravel, paved and unpaved surfaces: surfaces that will bring you closer to the actual conditions likely to be encountered in a real emergency.

The responses in this chapter are given in terms of one side, right or left, but in many instances the other side may be practiced by simply reversing the instructions.

Finally, bear in mind that in an encounter with armed assailants you may not come out unscathed, even though you achieve victory; that often when you are faced with a beating by club or stick it is better to offer some easily borne "target" than a vital one. For example, it is better to suffer a broken arm or hand than a head. He who manages to escape without any injury from conflict with an armed assailant is indeed skillful—or, more likely, just lucky. In facing the club or stick you have two choices. One is to get *outside* of the swing zone, the other to get *inside* of the swing zone. The immediate surroundings you find yourself in will often restrict you, leaving you only one choice. Regardless of your actions, *never* assume that your first response will satisfy the situation. Keep a constant vigilance that will enable you to continue your attack, should it become necessary. Target areas on the assailant's anatomy suggested by this book may be modified to meet your physical capabilities or limitations and you should try as many variations as you can devise.

OVERHEAD CLUB STRIKING

Situation: You are faced by an assailant who is holding a club in his right hand and who is closing in on you in an attempt to deliver an overhead striking attack. You have plenty of room to move around.

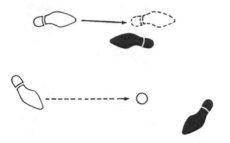

Response: Quickly face your assailant in a Forward Stance and a Half-front-facing Posture with your left foot advanced. As he closes in on you and prepares to strike you, drive hard off on your rear right leg and step deeply in with your left leg to meet him, placing your left foot to the outside of and slightly behind his advanced right foot. Refer to the diagram. Simultaneously, raise your arms in an upward X-block fashion, keeping your right arm inside your left arm. This action actually lunges your body forward directly into the assailant as your X-blocking action contacts upward hard against the underside of the assailant's right arm at a point near his wrist. His club-swinging right arm must be firmly wedged in the saddle formed by the crossing of your arms.

Quickly grasp the assailant's club arm with both hands, your thumbs facing each other, and pull his right arm downward to your right rear,

using the Grasping Block method. Begin to raise your right foot off the ground, bending your knee and bringing your thigh parallel to the ground. This action can be seen from another angle in the illustrations below.

Execute a hard Front Snap Kick, using the ball of your right foot or the point of your shoe, to the assailant's midsection, groin, knee, or shin, as you use the Grasping Block to unbalance him forward. This action can be seen on the next page.

Key Points: Your lunge action, stepping close into the assailant, must be performed fast and with your chest held high to give your X-block power. Time your Grasping Block action with this step-in action, using a twist of your hips to the right to reinforce your pull downward. Deliver your Snap Kick with a short action, not a long, looping movement.

20

DIAGONAL CLUB STRIKING

Situation: You are faced by an assailant who is holding a club in his right hand and who is closing in on you in an attempt to deliver a downward diagonal striking attack. You have plenty of room to move around.

Response: Face your assailant using a Forward Stance in a Half-front-facing Posture, with your left foot advanced. As he swings the club diagonally downward against your left arm, quickly withdraw that arm. Your assailant now attacks with a hard downward swing at your left knee. Keeping your rear foot in place, push away from your advanced left foot and bring your weight fully onto your rear right leg, lifting your left leg out of range of the assailant's club.

As the assailant's club misses your left leg, quickly step your left foot forward just inside of the assailant's advanced left foot. Simultaneously with that stepping action, swing your left arm across your body, in a Downward Block, hard into the club arm of the assailant, contacting his arm at any point below his elbow. Simultaneously twist your hips to your right and bring your right fist alongside your right hip, knuckles downward. As your Downward Block contacts the assailant's club arm, apply the Pressing Block to keep his club arm inactive. Shift your weight onto your advanced left foot as you do this.

Deliver a hard Elbow Forward Strike to the face or head of the assailant, using your right arm by twisting your hips forward as you strike. This action can be seen on the next page.

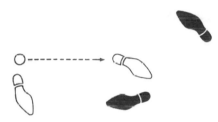

Key Points: After avoiding the assailant's downward diagonal striking action aimed at your left leg, step your left foot so that your toes point to your right and not straight forward. If during delivery of your Elbow Forward Strike the assailant breaks contact and steps away, you may step forward with your right foot to close the gap and allow you to hit the target.

BACKHAND CLUB STRIKING

Situation: You are confronted by an assailant who is holding a club in his right hand and who is closing in on you in an attempt to deliver a backhand striking action against you. You have plenty of room to move around.

Response: Quickly take the Forward Stance with a Half-front-facing Posture, with your right foot advanced. At the assailant's backhand swing, which is aimed at your head, duck forward, under, and to the right. This ducking action is inside of the club swing, or toward the inside of his swinging arm. Refer to the diagram. Get low and, as your head passes under the assailant's swing, throw your left arm upward, hand held in a tight fist, in Rising Block style. Withdraw your right arm, hand held in a tight fist, along your right side.

As the assailant reswings at your head, stop his arm with your left arm, using the Rising Block position, coordinating this with a stepping action of your left foot to a position as shown in the diagram. Quickly grasp the assailant's club arm with your left hand at any point below his elbow, snapping his club arm slightly outward and downward as you straighten your body and begin to drive your right elbow into his midsection.

Deliver a hard Elbow Forward Strike to your assailant's midsection, maintaining your left-hand grasp on his club arm. This action can be seen on the next page.

Key Points: The ducking action of your head is critical. It is not the type of simple head action in which you move your head backward, or down and under. Study the diagram on page 23 carefully and note that to perform this action you must move your hips circularly as you swing your upper body forward and around to your right. If the assailant steps back to break contact with you, you may step in with your right foot as you deliver your Elbow Forward Strike to his midsection, or you may keep your feet in place and deliver a Forefist or Hand Spear to his face or throat area.

HAYMAKER STICK SWING

Situation: An assailant is closing in on you with a stick held in his right hand. He is attempting to swing a haymaker at you, using the stick against your head. You have a limited amount of room in which to move.

Response: Face your assailant in a left Forward Stance using a Half-front-facing Posture. As he swings his stick in haymaker fashion, aiming at your head, raise your left arm, holding your hand in Knife-hand fashion. Withdraw your right arm, hand held in a tight fist, knuckles down, along your right side. Step your left foot circularly forward as shown in the diagram to a position just inside of the assailant's advanced left foot. Simultaneously with this stepping action, bring your right hand, held open, up alongside your head above your right shoulder. At the same time deliver a Knife-hand Block with your left hand hard against the inside of the assailant's stick arm at any point near his wrist.

Deliver a hard Knife-hand Strike to the assailant's side of the neck or head with your right hand, timing this blow with your stepping action and a twist of your hips to the left. With your left hand grasp the assailant's stick arm. This action can be seen on the opposite page. When the assailant has crowded too close to permit effective use of the Knife-hand Strike, drive a hard Elbow Forward Strike, using your right arm, into the assailant's midsection directly from the first position shown above. This action can be seen on page 32.

30

Key Points: Notice that your stepping-in action as well as the left Knife-hand Block, which must be executed in coordination with the step, are circular movements. Neither is a straight action. However, your right-hand Knife-hand Strike is straight to the target and is reinforced by the twist of your hips to the left and a slight lowering of your hips as you hit the target. You must pull the stick arm of the assailant with your left hand to unbalance him forward.

OVERHEAD STICK STRIKING

Situation: You are facing an assailant who is threatening to strike you with a stick in a two-handed overhead action. You have a limited amount of room in which to move.

Response: Face the assailant in a left Forward Stance with Half-front-facing Posture. At the downward stroke of the assailant's swing, quickly step forward and drive the palms of your hands hard upward underneath his arms, contacting them at points just at or slightly below his elbows. This is a special use of the Palm-heel Block in which both hands are used and it is an exception to the standard employment of the Palm-heel. Push hard upward against the assailant's arms to stop his overhead striking action. Quickly apply an unbalancing action, using your left

hand to push the assailant's right arm outward to your right and your right arm to push the assailant's left arm inward to your left. This action will bend the assailant's body forward and give you a chance to place a powerful kneeing attack.

Deliver a hard Front Knee Kick to the assailant's midsection or groin regions with your right knee as you pull him downward and to your right rear with both your hands. This action can be seen on the next page.

Key Points: Your forward-stepping action must be performed with your chest held high. Drive your Palm-heel Block circularly upward with your thumbs inward, catching the force of the blows on the heel portions of your hands. After contact, grasp hard and apply a "steering" action to the assailant's arms, as if turning hard to your right. Coordinate your "steering" action and downward pull of your hands to your right rear corner with your kneeing action.

36

LOW SWING STICK STRIKING

Situation: An assailant is closing in on you with a stick held in both hands and prepared for an attack at your lower body. You have a limited amount of room in which to move about.

Response: Face your assailant in a Forward Stance and a Half-front-facing Posture, advancing your foot that is on the side from which the assailant is swinging the stick (left foot shown advanced). Square off with your left hand held open and your right hand held in a tight fist, knuckles down, at your right side. As the assailant swings his low blow at your body (leg area shown), step in circularly with your left foot to meet him as shown in the diagram, allowing your right foot to follow normally to maintain balance. Drive a hard Knife-hand Strike into the assailant's stick arm at any point below his right elbow, using the motion

of the Downward Block with your left arm. Simultaneously with this blocking and striking action, straighten your body and begin to drive a Palm-heel direct to the assailant's face with your right hand. In executing this Palm-heel Strike, when necessary, step a bit forward with your right foot as you twist your hips to the left.

Deliver a hard Palm-heel Strike to the jaw or facial area of the assailant as you grasp his stick arm with your left hand and pull him forward to unbalance him. This action can be seen on the next page.

39

Key Points: Notice that your original stepping action with your left foot is not a straight-in action but that it traces a circular path. If you do not grasp the assailant's stick arm with your left hand after blocking, you must keep some kind of contact to ward off any additional stick striking attempts by him until you can get your Palm-heel to the target.

40

BACKHAND STICK SWING

Situation: An assailant has run you into a corner, giving you little room to move backward, and is preparing to backhand you with a stick held in his right hand.

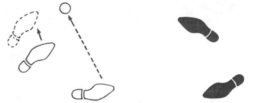

Response: Face the assailant in a Forward Stance with a Front-facing Posture, advancing the leg on the side where the stick is being held (right foot shown advanced). As the assailant starts his backhand swing, step away from the blow, shifting your right foot as shown above. Bend your upper body away from the blow as you bend your left leg, lower your hips and bring your right leg, knee bent, close to your body, thigh parallel to the ground. As the assailant's stick misses you, place both your hands on the ground to aid your balance and drive the heel of your right foot hard straight backward, parallel to the ground and into the assailant's groin. As an alternate action, you may keep your position as shown in the second illustration above, and deliver a hard Foot Edge to the assailant's knee or shin as shown on the opposite page.

After either kicking action, quickly return your right foot to the ground, placing it close to the assailant, and deliver a hard Forefist direct to the assailant's facial area (jaw) with your left hand by twisting your hips to the right, pivoting your feet in place, and turning your body to the assailant (see diagram). This action can be seen on page 44.

42

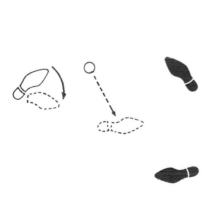

Key Points: Avoiding the backhand stick swing is essential. Even when you lean away to avoid the swing you may get hit on the trunk or right leg, but, if you lean away properly, the blow will not be strong enough to stop you from attacking with your kicking action and final Forefist action. In your final Forefist Strike, withdraw your right arm along your right side, hand held in a tight fist, knuckles downward, in anticipation of continuing your attack against the assailant when necessary.

STICK RAKING ATTACK

Situation: You are facing an assailant who holds a stick in both hands and who is preparing to use it in quarter-staff raking style against your midsection or groin. You have sufficient room in which to move.

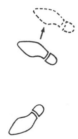

Response: Stand in a Forward Stance using the Half-front-facing Posture. Try to anticipate which end of the stick will be used and advance the foot on that side (left shown). As the assailant drives forward with the stick, blend with his attack motion by sidestepping to your right with your right foot as shown in the diagram. Using the Sweeping Block method, misdirect the stick to your rear and catch it firmly with your left hand. Simultaneously, shift your weight to your right leg, bending it at the knee, and raise your left leg close to your body, thigh parallel to the ground, foot tucked in close. Pull the assailant off balance with your left hand and deliver a hard Foot Edge direct to the assailant's knee or shin with your left foot.

46

Immediately after this kicking action, place your left foot close alongside the assailant's advanced right foot and, maintaining your left-hand grasp on the stick, deliver a hard Hand Spear direct to the assailant's facial area, coordinating this striking action with a twist of your hips to the left. This action can be seen on the next page.

Key Points: Blend with the assailant's attack motion and, as you apply your Sweeping Block, do not try to stop his stick thrust, but brush the attack to your rear. This action will off-balance him and prevent you from getting a wrist injury. Grasp his stick close to his right hand with your left hand and maintain this grasp while you kick and deliver your final Hand Spear counterattack.

TWO-HANDED DIAGONAL STICK STRIKING

Situation: You are caught almost unaware by an assailant who is delivering a two-handed stick attack against your head. There is no time to move to escape the attack although there is sufficient room in which to move.

Response: You are caught in the right Forward Stance with a Front-facing Posture by the assailant, who tries to bring his stick down on top of your head. Throw up your right arm, using the hand in Knife-hand-block fashion against the stick, thus warding off the intended blow. Simultaneously catch the lower end of the assailant's stick, near where he is gripping, with your left hand, held palm upward. Step your left rear foot quickly forward to a point in front of and at right angles to the assailant's left rear foot. Diagram shows this relationship. With this stepping action, turn the stick with your hands close to the assailant's body, bringing the lower end of his stick, held in your left hand, up and

over to your right as your right hand, holding the upper end of his stick, pulls downward and circularly inward. The illustrations below show this stick-turning action from another advantageous angle.

Continue turning the stick and drive your body forward against the assailant as you twist him into his rear left corner and wrench the stick out of his hands. This final stage can be seen on the next page.

Key Points: Catch the stick on the heels of your hands to avoid injury to your hands. You must turn the stick close to the assailant's body, coordinating the turn and your stepping action. Do not let your arms widen during the turning of the stick, but try to keep your elbows close to your body. At any stage after you catch the stick, you may deliver a kicking attack by using the ball of your foot or the tip of your shoe to the shin or knee of the assailant, or you may drive your knee into his groin. After wrenching the stick away from your assailant, be prepared for a continuation of his attack.

52

STICK PUSHING ATTACK

Situation: You are facing an assailant who is using his stick in quarter-staff pushing fashion, trying to press against your upper body or neck in an attempt to drive you into a corner and subdue you. You have plenty of room to move about.

Response: Face your assailant in a Forward Stance and a Half-front-facing Posture. Advance one foot so that it is just opposite to his rear foot (your left foot shown advanced). At the assailant's pushing attack, pivot inward a bit on your right foot as you bring your left foot around deep behind you, as shown in the diagram. While executing these foot actions, bring your hands up in front of you, the left hand held palm forward and the right hand held palm upward. As you catch the assailant's stick with both hands, lunge your body slightly forward to give resistance against his pushing.

After grasping the stick, don't try to pull it out of the assailant's hands, but, keeping a firm grip, pivot your right foot inward once more and bring your left foot circularly around behind you, as shown in the diagram. Twist your hips to your left, lowering them a bit. This action may make the assailant step forward with his right foot, but, whether he does so or not, your actions remain the same. As you pivot, step and twist your hips, your right hand driving upward and over as your left hand pulls downward and in on the stick, thus turning it in a short circle.

Continue turning the stick and drive your body forward in the direction of your hand action as you twist him into his front right corner and wrench the stick out of his hands. This can be seen on the next page.

Key Points: Catch the stick on the heels of your hands to avoid injury to your hands. You must not tug to pull the stick away from the assailant, but instead, pivot in front of him and turn the stick with a circular action close to your body. Do not widen your arms during this turning of the stick, but seek to keep your elbows close to your body. At any stage after catching the stick you may deliver a kicking attack, using the ball of your foot or the tip of your shoe to the shin, knee, or groin of the assailant, or you may use your Foot Edge to stamp on his arch.

CLOSE STICK STRUGGLE

Situation: You have been surprised by an assailant who is holding a stick in both hands and who attempts to strike you with it. You have made a successful catch of the stick with both hands and have sufficient room to move about.

57

Response: You are in a right Forward Stance with the Front-facing Posture as you catch the stick with both hands, left-hand palm held forward and right-hand palm held upward. Pull the stick a bit to get the assailant to pull back against you. Step your right foot directly forward and to a position behind your assailant's right foot, as shown in the diagram. Simultaneously with this stepping action, apply a turning action to the assailant's stick, your right hand driving hard upward and over as your left hand pulls downward and in.

58

Lunge your body hard forward into the assailant's rear right corner as you turn the stick, bracing yourself with a strong push from your left rear foot.

Bend your assailant over backward as you continue your turning action against the stick until he topples backward and the stick is wrenched from his grasp. This action can be seen on the next page.

Key Points: Your turning action against the stick is a short circular action that turns the stick almost in place. Do not let your arms widen during this turning movement, but seek to keep your elbows close to your body. Lower your hips as you drive your assailant to the ground. Keep alert for a continuation of his attack after you take the stick away from him.

Chapter Two
BLADE AND SHARP-EDGE ATTACKS

BLADED and other sharp-edged instruments in the hands of assailants are often used for making overhead, backhand, diagonal, or haymaker strokes as well as in jabbing, thrusting, and blocking tactics. Combinations of slashing and stabbing methods can be used with deadly effect against untrained persons.

The assailant wielding a bladed or sharp-edged object must be treated with extreme caution and makes it necessary for you to make the proper response if you are to avoid serious injury or the taking of your life. Like club and stick attacks, the situations are complex, but unlike the methods of the club and stick, bladed and sharp-edged weapons present a more dangerous set of conditions that make it absolutely necessary for you not to make any mistakes in defense responses.

Karate experts can face blade and sharp-edge attacks with confidence, *but never without difficulty*. You as the average citizen must develop appropriate responses as described in this chapter. They have been designed for your use and include the necessary principles to better meet common eventualities connected with armed single assailants.

All responses outlined in this chapter should be practiced with a partner. Gain complete knowledge of what you are trying to do by having the attack made slowly at first, gradually working up to an automatic response at high speed. Frequent practice, several days per week will greatly aid your development.

Use your daily dress in all practices and do not confine yourself to flat, smooth surfaces such as a gym floor. Practice on grass, gravel, paved and unpaved surfaces, thus making your practice sessions closer to the actual conditions likely to happen in real life.

All responses in this chapter are shown in terms of one side, either right or left, but in most instances the other side may be learned by simply reversing the instructions.

Bear in mind these final words concerning conflict with assailants armed with bladed or sharp-edged weapons. Like encounters with assailants armed with clubs or sticks, it is difficult to come out with no injury to yourself and it may be necessary to offer some "target" as bait while you protect more vital areas and make a successful defense. Here too you have two choices. Either get *inside* of the swing zone or get *outside* of it. Often your surroundings will force you into one or the other pattern, but regardless of what you do, do it with the attitude that perhaps your first response *will not* satisfy the situation. Keep a constant vigilance that will enable you to continue your attack, should it become necessary. Vary the target areas suggested in this chapter and seek to improve your effectiveness, keeping in mind that the weapon-bearing assailant need not be treated with conservative kindness. He is after your life!

MIDSECTION KNIFE THRUST

Situation: An assailant is menacing you with a knife held in his right hand and is trying to stab you in the stomach. You have enough room to move around.

Response: Confront your assailant in a Forward Stance with a Front-facing Posture. Advance your leg on the side facing the knife (left leg shown advanced). As the assailant lunges forward and stabs at your midsection, turn your body to the right by simply stepping your right foot circularly to your rear, leaving your left foot in place. Simultaneously with this avoiding action, raise both your arms to about shoulder height and hold them, palms downward, in front of you. As the knife nears you, apply the Grasping Block by an inward pressing action of your left hand and a top gripping action of your right hand, driving the knife arm downward.

64

Take a firm grasp of the knife arm and pull it diagonally backward to your right rear corner (away from your body) and begin to shift your weight to your left foot as you lift your right leg from the ground, bending the knee so so that the thigh is parallel to the ground.

Deliver a hard Front Snap Kick, using the ball of your foot or the tip of your shoe direct to the assailant's groin or midsection. This action can be seen on the next page.

Key Points: Premature stepping to avoid the knife thrust is useless, and the timing necessary for proper avoiding action is critical. The Grasping Block must be correctly performed and requires you to retain a strong grip in order that you may unbalance the assailant as you deliver your kick as well as to aid your balance during kicking.

DIAGONAL DOWNWARD KNIFE SLASH

Situation: An assailant is menacing you by closing in on you as he holds a knife in his right hand near his right shoulder, blade upward. You have plenty of room to move around.

Response: Keep alert and, as the assailant begins his slashing action, drive a Rising Block hard against his knife hand at any point near his mid-forearm, using your left arm. It may be necessary to step in close to the assailant to do this. If so, step your left foot circularly forward to a point just along the inside of the assailant's advanced right foot. Allow your right foot to follow normally (see diagram).

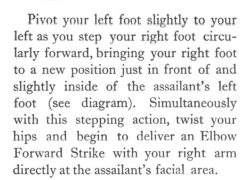

Pivot your left foot slightly to your left as you step your right foot circularly forward, bringing your right foot to a new position just in front of and slightly inside of the assailant's left foot (see diagram). Simultaneously with this stepping action, twist your hips and begin to deliver an Elbow Forward Strike with your right arm directly at the assailant's facial area.

Deliver a hard Elbow Forward Strike to the assailant's face as you lower your hips slightly and grasp the assailant's knife arm with your left hand at a point near his wrist. This action can be seen on the next page.

Key Points: Your stepping action may only be necessary if the assailant has not closed in with you but has begun his slashing action. Regardless of whether you step in or not, you must get *inside* the slashing blade. Notice that as you apply your Rising Block your right arm is withdrawn alongside your right side, hand held in a tight fist, knuckles down.

OVERHEAD KNIFE STABBING ATTACK

Situation: Your assailant is closing in on you, holding a knife in his right hand in preparation for an overhead stabbing attack. You have plenty of room to maneuver.

Response: Face the assailant in a Forward Stance with a Front-facing Posture, advancing the leg on the side of his knife hand (left leg shown advanced). As the assailant closes in and lunges at you, bringing the knife downward aimed at stabbing you, sidestep quickly to your left by stepping your left foot directly to your left as in the diagram. As you sidestep, bend your left knee and bend your body away from the downward motion of the knife. Carry your right leg, thigh parallel to the ground, close to your body, centering your full weight on your left foot. Keep your eyes on the assailant's knife.

72

Simultaneously, use your right hand in a Sweeping Block fashion, directing it against the outside of the assailant's knife arm at any point along his arm. This action misdirects the assailant's downward stabbing attack and knocks it away from being in line with your body. At the same instant, deliver a hard Foot Edge to the assailant's right knee joint, using your right foot.

Immediately grasp the assailant's knife arm near the wrist, using your right hand, and at the same time step your right foot down behind the assailant's right foot. Keeping your feet more or less in place, pivot on your feet and twist your hips to the right and deliver an outside Knife-hand to the base of the assailant's skull with your left hand. This action can be seen on the next page.

Key Points: Your sidestepping action is critical. If it is too soon, your assailant can easily follow you with his stabbing action. Be sure to bend your body away from the knife's path but do not overbend to your left as you will lose your balance and weaken your Foot Edge kick attack. Your Foot Edge kick may be directed against any angle of the assailant's knee. Seek to blend your movements of kick, stepping of your right foot, hip twist, and delivery of the outside Knife-hand into a smooth sequence.

74

SWITCHING HANDS KNIFE ATTACK

Situation: Your assailant is cautiously closing in on you with a shuffle step while holding a knife in his right hand and making short test slashes or stabs at your midsection with his right hand. Suddenly he switches the knife to his left hand and makes a lunge-stab at your midsection. You have plenty of room to move around.

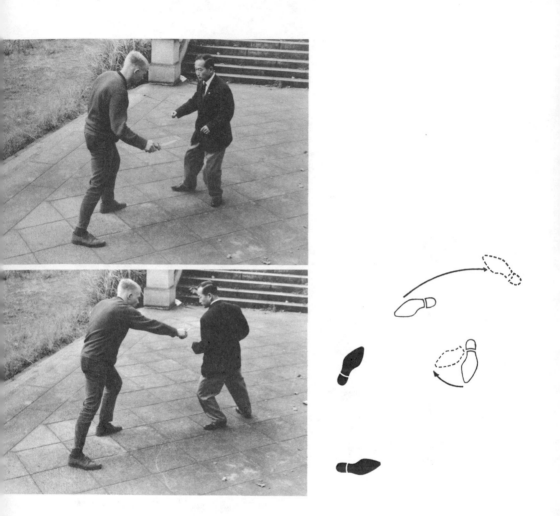

Response: Face your assailant in a right Forward Stance with a Front-facing Posture, keeping both of your hands, held as tight fists, in front of you. As your assailant stabs or slashes at you with the knife in his right hand, avoid his action by pivoting your body backward *outside* the knife's range by taking a circular step backward with your right foot and pivoting your left foot a bit to your right as shown in the diagram. This action turns your body out of the knife's range and places you in a left Forward Stance with a Half-front-facing Posture.

Your assailant now quickly switches his knife to his left hand in order to slash or stab at you more effectively. Keep your balance and keep your eyes on his knife hand (left now). Anticipate his lunge forward, keeping your body weight primarily on your right foot and holding your hands, held as tight fists, in front of you but close to your body.

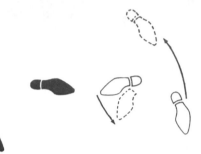

At the assailant's lunge, quickly pivot your body backward in a large circular motion by swinging your left foot around behind you and allowing your right foot to pivot a bit to your left as shown in the diagram. Simultaneously with this body-pivot action, swing your right arm circularly around and block hard against the assailant's thrusting knife arm with the top of your forearm or its outer edge. Immediately withdraw your left hand alongside your left hip, holding your hand in a tight fist, knuckles downward. This action can be seen from another angle in the illustrations below. Note that it may be necessary to step into the assailant a bit with your right foot to make a strong blocking contact.

By this action you are *inside* of the knife's range, and your next operations are critical. Grasp the assailant's knife arm (left) near the wrist with your left hand. Lower your hips at the same time to keep your balance. Quickly fold your right arm high across your chest, with your fist near your left shoulder, held tightly, knuckles down. Continue your left-hand grasping action, pulling hard against the assailant's left knife hand, bringing him off balance on a line extended downward from his knife arm. The illustrations on this page show this critical moment.

Strike the assailant hard in his facial or head area by delivering a fast Back Fist, Bottom Fist, or Knife-hand with a snap of your right arm. This action can be seen on the next page.

Key Points: Your evasive body pivotal actions are very necessary to make this response safe and functional. They must be the result of your entire body turning as a unit, not separating feet, hips, and upper body as you move. The pivotal actions must be accurately timed with the knifing actions of your assailant and not come prematurely or too late if you are to avoid injury.

LAPEL SEIZURE AND KNIFE STAB ATTACK

Situation: An assailant has grasped your lapel (right or left) with his right hand and is threatening to stab you with a knife held in his left hand. You have ample room to move about.

Response: Upon being grabbed by the assailant, quickly pivot your body to your right and bring your left shoulder hard against the lapel-grasping arm of your assailant. Simultaneously with this pivotal action of your body, drive a hard Palm-heel Block with your left hand, downward against the assailant's knife arm at a point near his wrist. Use a minimum of footwork, as shown in the diagram, to aid your

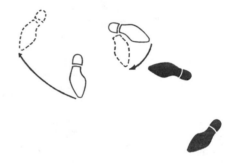

body to escape any stabbing action by the assailant, and withdraw your right hand alongside your right hip, hand held in a tight fist, knuckles downward, as you pivot. Immediately start to drive a hard Hand Spear into the eyes or throat of the assailant, using your right hand as you twist your body to the left and face your assailant.

During the delivery of your Hand Spear, your left hand continues to apply a Palm-heel Block action, but upon completion of the Hand Spear Strike to the target, quickly deliver a hard Elbow Forward Strike to the assailant's right rib or kidney areas, using your left arm. As you strike, lower your hips by stepping into the assailant with your left foot and twisting your body to your right as you withdraw your right arm alongside your body, hand at your right hip and held in a tight fist, knuckles downward, where it is ready to continue your attack. This action can be seen on the next page.

Key Points: Your initial use of your shoulder against the assailant's grasping right arm is of vital importance. Your whole body must unite to make this blocking and evasive action effective.

84

UPPERCUT KNIFE SLASH ATTACK

Situation: An assailant is closing in on you, carrying a knife low in his right hand, point toward you, threatening to use it in an uppercut slash fashion. You are backing up on rough terrain and you slip and fall down trying to avoid the knife. You have ample room to maneuver.

Response: You are backing up, keeping a right Forward Stance with a Front-facing Posture. As your assailant makes his uppercut slash attack, you quickly change into a right Back Stance with a Half-front-facing Posture to avoid the slash by shifting your weight onto your rear left leg and bending that knee. Your quick weight shift causes you to lose your balance and you fall to the ground at the feet of your assailant. Try your best to fall onto your left hip and support yourself with your left hand on the ground, fingers pointing in toward your body, not away from you. Your left leg is bent at the knee and folded underneath you. Keep your eyes on the assailant.

Draw your right leg up to your body so that your knee is close to your chest and drop your body weight farther away from the assailant by bending your left arm as much as necessary (even placing the elbow on the ground if necessary). Keep your right hand ready near your right knee. Your assailant's uppercut slashing action has missed the target and as this will bring a new attack action from him, you must be very alert. As the assailant turns the point of his knife over and downward to attempt a stabbing attack at you as you lie on the ground, raise your body slightly so that you come in closer to him. Use your left arm to aid you. Keep your right leg slightly bent but more forward to

aid in keeping your balance and bringing you up to meet the assailant's attack.

As the stabbing attack is delivered downward at you, use your free right hand in Palm-heel Block fashion to deflect the knife hand, catching it instantly with that hand. Pull his knife arm downward with a snap and deliver a hard Foot Edge with your right leg direct to his shin or knee. This action can be seen on this page. Immediately after delivering

your Foot Edge, continue pulling the assailant's knife arm hard downward. Push yourself up to a kneeling position with your left hand or by
using the assailant's resistance backwards to achieve this.

As your weight shifts forward and your left hand becomes free,
form a tight fist and deliver a hard Fore Fist directly to the assailant's
groin, rib, or solar-plexus area. This action can be seen on the next
page.

Key Points: When you lose balance, do your best to fall down on a line with an extension of the line through your feet. *Do not* sit down directly backwards. Your falling down is more of a reclining action than a sitting one. To do this easily and with some balance, you must keep your left leg drawn up under you as you go down. Another thing to keep in mind is that your left hand, which will become your support hand, must be placed with the fingers pointing *toward* you, not away from you. Place your left support hand on the same line of extension as your feet and the direction of falling.

90

KNIFE FACE THRUST ATTACK

Situation: An assailant is stalking you with a knife held in his right hand, point toward you. He is making straight thrusts at your upper body and face. You have plenty of room to move around in.

Response: Face your assailant in the left Forward Stance with a Front-facing Posture. Move so as to keep just outside of the assailant's thrust range, shifting to the Back Stance, if necessary, when the assailant thrusts. Quickly take this opportunity to shift your full weight to your rear right leg, knee bent, as you deliver a hard Front Snap Kick, using the tip of your left shoe, to the assailant's knife arm at any point along the arm.

Immediately after delivering your kicking action, return your left leg so that your thigh is parallel to the ground and then step that leg deeply toward the assailant to a point outside of and slightly behind the assailant's advanced right foot. See diagram. Simultaneously with this stepping action, drive a hard blocking action to the assailant's knife arm, using your left arm (or hand) in either Rising Block or Knife-hand Block fashion at a point near the assailant's wrist. Following this, withdraw your right arm alongside your body, hand held in a Hand Spear at your right hip. As your blocking action takes effect, catch the assailant's knife arm near his wrist with your left hand and pull his knife arm hard downward with a snap as you begin to deliver a fast Hand Spear direct to the assailant's throat or eye areas. This final action can be seen on the next page.

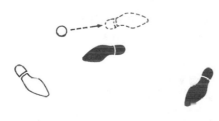

Key Points: Your body weight shift must bring you out of range of the knife thrust and place you in the Back Stance in order for you to free your left leg for kicking and stepping actions. If the kicking action is impossible for you (due to restrictions of your body or clothes), move directly from the Back Stance into the left blocking and right Spear Hand actions without kicking. Step deep enough to bring you into effective blocking range.

BROKEN BOTTLE FREE THREAT
TO MIDSECTION

Situation: You are being menaced by an assailant holding a broken bottle in his left hand. He is moving in on you and thrusting at your midsection. You have sufficient room to move about.

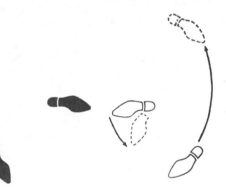

Response: Face your assailant in a right Forward Stance with a Front-facing Posture. Shuffle backward, always keeping outside of his thrust attack. At one of his thrusts, avoid it by turning your body out of range to the rear. Do this by pivoting slightly to your left with your right foot and swinging your left foot around behind you in a circular manner. See diagram. Simultaneously with this action, raise your right arm, your hand held high above your head in a Knife Hand, and withdraw your left arm alongside your left hip, hand held in a tight fist, knuckles downward.

As you come into place in the new position, quickly deliver a hard Knife-hand against the bottle arm of the assailant at a point near his wrist, using your right hand in a snapping motion. Immediately shift your weight forward onto your right leg and catch the assailant's bottle arm with your left hand, palm downard, at any point near his wrist. Fold your now free right arm across your chest parallel to the ground, holding your hand in a tight fist, knuckles upward.

Drive a hard Bottom or Back Fist direct to the assailant's face or head area, using your right hand. This action can be seen on the next page.

Key Points: Your turning action to avoid his thrust must be a unified action of your whole body. When you strike with your Knife Hand against the assailant's bottle arm, lower your hips with the contact. If necessary, step into the assailant with your right foot as you deliver your final striking action.

98

BROKEN BOTTLE FREE THREAT TO FACE

Situation: An assailant is threatening to thrust a broken bottle into your face. He is holding it with his right hand. You have a limited amount of room to move about.

Response: Take the right Forward Stance with a Half-front-facing Posture and keep your hands ready in front of you as the assailant gets set to attack. At his thrust, shift your weight to your left rear corner as you step backward and slightly sideward with your left foot. Bring your weight well onto your left foot in this new position so as to move your body out of line of the bottle thrust. As you perform this weight shift and stepping action, twist your body to your left and raise your right arm, folding it across your body parallel to the ground, hand held in a tight fist near your left shoulder, knuckles outward, and withdraw your left arm close alongside your body, hand held in a tight fist at your left hip, knuckles downward.

Quickly deliver a hard Bottom or Back Fist to the assailant's bottle arm at any point below the elbow of that arm, using your right hand in a snapping fashion. Keep you left fist ready at your left hip.

Immediately upon completion of your Bottom or Back Fist striking action, twist your hips to a Front-facing Posture as you deliver a hard left Fore Fist into the assailant's rib area or solar plexus. This action can be seen on the next page.

Key Points: Weight shifting is essential here. The initial avoiding action is a weight shift to your left rear corner *out of range* of the bottle thrust. Your second weight shift carries you back *into range* for blocking and striking. Note the flex in the knees during these actions.

102

BROKEN BOTTLE FREE THREAT TO FACE
(alternate method)

Situation: An assailant is closing in on you, thrusting a broken bottle, held in his right hand, at your face. You have no room to move backward.

Response: Face the assailant in a left Forward Stance using a Front-facing Posture. At the thrust, aimed at your face, bend your knees, drop your hips and sink down under the line of thrust, keeping your body upright and shifting your weight onto your rear right leg. Throw your hands upward in front of you to meet the thrust from underneath in X-block fashion with your left hand ahead of your right. Immediately duck your head and shift your weight forward onto your advanced left leg as you make blocking contact. Notice that your head moves in a dipping circular entry pattern. This action can also be seen in the illustrations below.

Catch the assailant's bottle arm near the wrist with your right hand and, as your left hand is freed, begin to make a tight fist with your left hand. Simultaneously step in deeply toward your assailant, with your left foot coming to rest outside of but slightly behind the assailant's right foot, and deliver a hard Bottom Fist directly to your assailant's rib areas or solar plexus with your left hand. At the same time pull hard with your right hand on the assailant's bottle arm. This striking action can be seen in the figure on the next page.

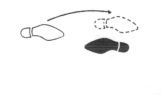

Key Points: Your entry under the bottle thrust must be curved as shown in the diagram. Use your rear right leg to push hard and launch yourself forward. Always keep your body upright, chest high. Coordinate your blocking action and catching action, and pull hard against the assailant's bottle arm as you deliver your Bottom Fist.

LAPEL SEIZURE AND BROKEN BOTTLE
FACE SLASH

Situation: An assailant has grabbed your right lapel with his left hand and is threatening to slash your face with a broken bottle he is holding in his right hand. You are able to move around a bit.

Response 1: At the assailant's grasp, take the right Forward Stance with a Front-facing Posture and keep alert for the coming attack to your face. At the attack, quickly twist your hips to the left but keep your feet in place. Use your left hand in either Rising Block (shown) or Sweeping Block fashion hard against the inside of the assailant's bottle arm, using a circular blocking action to your left rear.

Immediately after making blocking contact, step back with your left foot as shown in the diagram, pivoting your right foot to the left slightly, catching hold of the assailant's bottle arm near the wrist with your left hand and pulling it downward to your left rear in time with your back-stepping action. Simultaneously swing a hard right Fore Fist in roundhouse fashion over the assailant's grasping arm directly into his head or facial area. This action can be seen on the next page.

Key Points: Block, step, and twist your body in a circular manner. Do not use straight-line actions. Keep blocking contact at all times, but if the catching and pulling of the assailant's bottle arm is difficult or impossible, maintain a Pressing Block action.

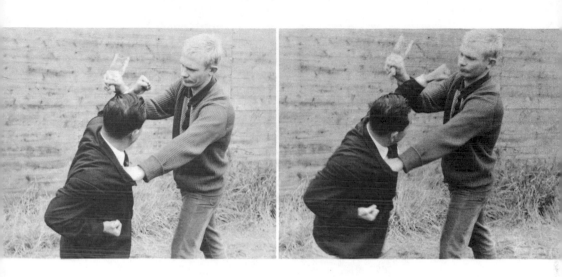

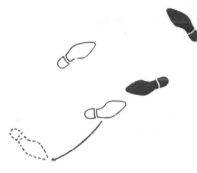

Response 2: At the assailant's grasp, take the left Forward Stance with a Front-facing Posture. At the moment of the slashing attack, quickly step backward with your right foot, lowering your hips a bit by bending your knees as you drive a hard left Rising Block against the inner and underside of the assailant's attacking bottle arm at any point near his wrist. Simultaneously withdraw your right arm alongside your body, hand held in a tight fist at your right hip, knuckles downward.

Immediately after blocking contact, deliver a hard left Fore Fist directly to the assailant's facial area by twisting your body still more to your right and withdrawing your right arm further alongside your body. Keep your right Fore Fist ready for continuation of the attack. This action can be seen on the next page.

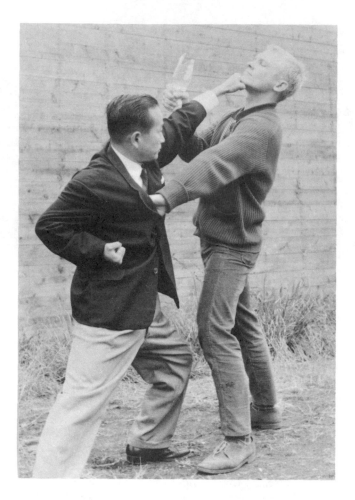

Key Points: The stepping, blocking, and striking actions in this response are all straight-line actions. After delivering your Fore Fist to the assailant's face, keep your left arm ready for further blocking action and use your right Fore Fist for any possible follow-up attack.

Chapter Three
MULTIPLE ARMED ASSAILANTS

ARMED assailants working in pairs or small groups commonly attack with methods that include overhead, backhand, diagonal, or haymaker swings, using club, stick, or sharp-edged instruments with stroking as well as jabbing, poking, and thrusting techniques in various combinations. All of these tactics are terribly effective against an untrained person. More often than not, assailants work in pairs or small groups with one or more unarmed members distracting the intended victim while one or more armed members of the group make the sneak attack. The situation can be reversed in which the armed assailant or assailants menace the intended victim until an unarmed sneak attack can be effected.

Being attacked by more than one assailant and in such a way as to involve a weapon requires a proper response if you hope to avoid serious injury or the taking of your life. The complexity of the situations is obvious and you can not afford to make even just one mistake.

Karate techniques well learned, as in the case of experts, allow such persons to meet the described situations with confidence, but, once again, *not without difficulty*. The responses in this chapter are developed for you, the average man, and cover only a minimum of situations. However, the representative examples will serve to show you that the responses found elsewhere in this text, as well as in Books Two and Three, can be chained together to form adequate defense measures against multiple armed assailants. Unfortunately, the space limitations of this text preclude an exhaustive treatment of other situations, and, therefore, the design of other situations and responses is left to the practitioner. This should not be too difficult for any reader who has followed and practiced the first three volumes of this series properly.

All responses shown in this short chapter must be practiced with partners. Begin with a slow-motion speed, working up to full speed "attack" situations with their appropriate responses. Seek to build an automatic reponse pattern by daily practice several days per week.

Use your normal daily clothes to practice. Do not limit your practice sessions to a smooth, flat surface such as found in a gym, but get out on the grass, gravel, paved and unpaved surfaces. Strive to bring reality closer to you, for reality may not be kind to you if and when an actual assault happens.

The responses in this chapter are given in terms of one side, right or left, but in both instances, the other side may be practiced by simply reversing the instructions.

Keep alert as long as the situation is dangerous to you. Your first response may not settle the issue and you must be prepared to continue your attack. Vary the target areas suggested by this chapter, making sure that they remain effective as targets for your defense actions. Remember that assailants attacking you in the fashion shown in this chapter are bent on doing you great harm. Do not give them the chance!

FRONT AND REAR STICK ATTACK

Situation: You are walking on rough terrain and are aware of two assailants. One is in full view to your front and in your path of walking, while the other is lurking nearby in a clump of bushes. The rear assailant is armed with a stick.

Response: As you attempt to pass the front assailant, he suddenly lashes out at you with a right-legged kick aimed at your midsection. Quickly step into the kick, advancing your left leg, dropping your hips, and keeping your body upright. Use both your hands in X-block fashion (left hand underneath) or your left arm in a Downward Block fashion, keeping your right hand near the blocking contact.

After blocking contact, quickly catch the assailant's kicking leg trouser with your right hand and pull his leg across your body to your

right rear corner as you shift your weight onto your advanced left leg. This action will free your right leg. Bend it so that your thigh comes parallel to the ground.

As you pull the assailant's kicking leg across your body, quickly deliver a hard Snap Kick with your right leg, using the ball of your foot or the point of your shoe, directly to the groin of the assailant from underneath him. This action can be seen above.

Anticipate the rear assailant's stick attack by quickly completing your forward kicking action to the front assailant, bending your right leg so that your thigh is once again parallel to the ground. Keep your right-hand grasp, pulling on the frontal assailant's former kicking leg. Keep your weight full on your left leg, bending the knee slightly and keeping your left ankle firm to aid your balance as you drop your body forward and deliver a hard backward kick, using your heel as a point of contact, direct to the rear assailant's shin, knee, groin, or midsection. This action can be seen on the next page.

Key Points: Your blocking action against the front assailant's kick must be done fron a balanced position, making sure you maintain your body upright. Your right-hand grasping and pulling action must be strongly maintained to unbalance the front assailant and to aid your balance in delivering the rear kick. Pivot on your hips to perform the rear kick.

Situation: You are walking along in rough terrain and are suddenly menaced by a front assailant who threatens to strike you. While you are watching for his attack you are garrotted from the rear by a second assailant who has been in hiding. You have plenty of room to move.

Response: At the garrotte action, tense your neck muscles and keep your balance as much as possible. Do not try to tug away from the noose around your neck. Keep your eye on the front assailant and, as he swings a haymaker right, block his arm from the left Forward Stance and Front-facing Posture, using the X-block (left hand ahead of the right).

Immediately after blocking, catch the assailant's right arm in your left hand and snap it downward. Simultaneously twist slightly to your left and shift your weight onto your rear right leg. This action frees your left leg. Immediately deliver a hard forward Snap Kick to the front assailant's shin, knee, or groin, using the ball of your left foot or the tip of that shoe. See lower figure on page 120.

Upon completion of your forward kicking attack, immediately step backward and slightly to your left side, with your left foot, as shown in the diagram. As your foot comes into place, twist hard to your left and deliver a hard Bottom Fist to the rear assailant's rib or groin area, using your left hand. This action can be seen on the next page.

Key Points: At the garrotting attack you must resist the temptation to tie up your hands with feeble attempts to pull the noose from your neck. Keep your balance and get rid of the front assailant first with hard kicking action. When you twist to deal with the rear assailant, pivot with your neck in place as the central pivotal point. This response is not suitable for garrotting attacks that employ fine wire or slender cord materials, but can be worked against ordinary attacks that use toweling, ties, wide cloth bands, and the like.